9788537225790

D1784351

SIR WALTER RALEGH
1554-1618

ABOVE: *A vision of Queen Elizabeth in triumph, attributed to Robert Peake and probably dating from 1601, the last year of her reign. The Queen appears as a goddess-like figure of eternal beauty surrounded by the great nobles of the court, the Knights of the Garter, who carry the canopy above the triumphal car on which she rides. The picture is probably a tribute to the Queen commissioned by the Earl of Worcester, her Master of the Horse, who appears below her as the other central figure. It also celebrates the recent marriage between Worcester's heir, Lord Herbert, and Lady Anne Russell, the two figures in white satin on the right. Ralegh lacked the status and influence of men such as Worcester but he made himself by his personality and achievements a leading figure in this cult of the Queen.*

BACK COVER: *Sir Walter Ralegh as naval commander. In the background is a picture of the action at Cadiz in 1596, with Ralegh's flagship leading the English fleet into battle against the Spanish. He wears a commander's sash on his left arm, and holds a walking stick—a reminder that during the battle he received a serious leg wound and walked with a limp for the rest of his life. The painting, attributed to Sir William Segar, is dated 1598 on the canvas, but the man it depicts is markedly older than the Ralegh portrayed with his son in 1602. It is possible that this portrait of Ralegh as a national hero was painted after his death.*

For if his valure once be mou2de, reuenge on them to take,
Which doe our foueraigne P2inces lawes, like beaftly beaftes fo2fake:
Tys not the cruell fto2my rage, no2 gathered fo2ce of thofe
No2 yet the crooked crabbtree lookes, of greafye glibbed foes,
Can make him to reuoke the thing, his hono2 hath p2etended
But that Dame Juftice muft p2oceede, 'gap2ft thofe that haue offended.

9

Fo2 Mars will fee the finall end, of trayt'rous waged warres,
To plucke the hartes of Rebells downe, that lately pearft the ftarres.
To yelde them guerdon fo2 defertes, by rigour of his blade,
And with the fame to gall their hartes, which fuch vp2o2es haue made.
Loe where it is in open fight, moft perfect to be feene
Which fheweth the fatall end aright, of rebells to our Queene.

HVMFRIDVS GILBERTVS MILES AVRATVS

Et

Quid Non

ABOVE: *Elizabeth's army puts the Irish rebels to flight, a woodcut illustrating John Derricke's poem* The Image of Ireland, *published in 1581. The Irish usually avoided pitched battles, in which they were at a disadvantage against the better-armed English, preferring raids and ambushes. Ralegh several times put his life at risk in such actions. In 1586, after the rebellion had been put down, great tracts of land were parcelled out among a fortunate few. Ralegh, by this time the Queen's favourite, received an exceptionally large holding at one third the usual rent, brought in tenants from the West Country, and within a few years was making a handsome profit.*

LEFT: *Sir Humphrey Gilbert, Ralegh's half-brother and his senior by some 15 years, helped him begin his career as seaman, coloniser and courtier. Gilbert was one of three sons Ralegh's mother had by her previous marriage with Otho Gilbert. He was in Elizabeth's service even before she became queen for his great aunt, Kate Ashley, was Elizabeth's governess and Gilbert was attached to the Princess's household. He became one of the pioneers of the Elizabethan colonisation of Ireland and America, but he was too cantankerous to win the Queen's favour. His death became a national legend. About to cross the Atlantic from Newfoundland, he insisted on remaining in the smallest ship in his fleet, and it was swamped in heavy seas.*

2

Sir Walter Ralegh

Peter Hammond

D uring his own lifetime Sir Walter Ralegh was one of the best-known men in England. Even in the expansive age of the Elizabethan Renaissance no one could match his versatility and energy, as courtier and parliamentarian, soldier, seaman and explorer, businessman and publicist, scientist and philosopher, historian and poet. With his death he became a national legend. Yet Ralegh's formative years are obscure. He was born probably in either 1552 or 1554, at Hayes Barton in the parish of East Budleigh, near Exmouth in Devon, the second son of the local squire. Nothing of the young Ralegh is recorded until 1569, when he went over to France, one of a band of gentlemen volunteers, to fight on the Protestant side in the Wars of Religion – an allegiance he was to maintain for the rest of his life. In 1572 he went up to Oriel College, Oxford, but did not stay to take his degree. In 1575 he enrolled at the Middle Temple in the Inns of Court, less to embark on a legal education than to enjoy London society while he awaited preferment at the court of Queen Elizabeth.

Ralegh's first opportunity to make his mark came through his half-brother, Sir Humphrey Gilbert. In 1578 Ralegh joined him in a scheme to explore and colonise the coast of North America. The other ships in Gilbert's fleet were

*   *   *

RIGHT: *Robert Dudley, Earl of Leicester, while Governor-General of the Netherlands 1584–85. Leicester was Ralegh's most important patron, whom he succeeded as the Queen's prime favourite. Elizabeth had been infatuated with her 'Sweet Robin', and even contemplated marriage when Leicester's wife Amy, who had a fatal illness, should die. But when Amy died suddenly in suspicious circumstances she had to accept that marriage was impossible. But he remained one of the Queen's leading councillors and Ralegh took care to keep his goodwill.*

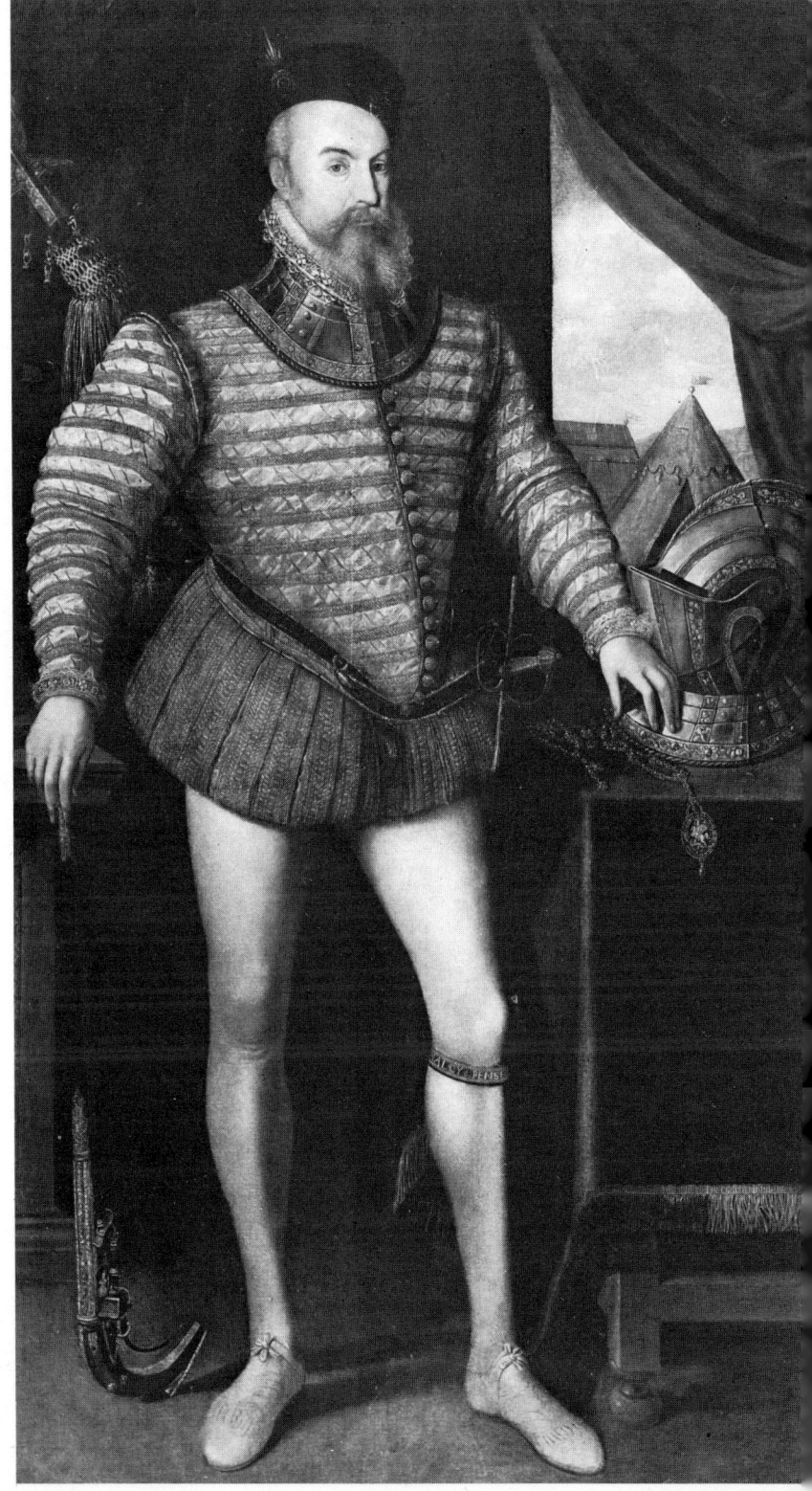

ABOVE: *The farm, or 'barton', of Hayes, near Budleigh Salterton on the south coast of Devon, where Ralegh was born. The Raleghs were an old Devon family, related to many of the leading gentry, but while Ralegh's father maintained his rank he was far from wealthy. Hayes Barton is the home of a prosperous yeoman rather than the local squire, and it was not even the elder Ralegh's property but was held on lease. When his son had established himself at Court, he tried to buy Hayes Barton, without success. The house remains largely unchanged and the family arms can still be seen on a window panel in the room where Ralegh was born.*

RIGHT: *Ralegh, 'the Queen's dear minion', painted by Elizabeth's miniaturist Nicholas Hilliard about 1585. Ralegh was famous for the rich elegance of his dress, even in his early days at Court when he had only modest means. Here he wears a great wheel-ruff edged with lace and a bonnet 'Henri Trois', a style borrowed from the French Court, with a bandeau entwined with a double row of pearls and a star-shaped jewel securing the white feather. The face surrounded by such fashionable extravagance is mature, resolute and commanding. From the beginning Ralegh was known, and disliked, for his pride.*

4

LEFT: *Elizabeth portrayed as the Virgin Queen by Sir William Segar, 1585. The ermine, on the Queen's right wrist, is a symbol of chastity. Elizabeth herself chose the name of Virginia for Ralegh's new colony in America, which was founded in that year. Here, as in the other portraits of her, the Queen appears as a cult-figure, her features idealised, her costume and the setting full of symbolism and allegory.*

BELOW: *An Indian of Virginia. The expedition sent out by Ralegh in 1584 returned with two Indians whom he presented to the Queen. They provided useful publicity for the colonising venture Ralegh was then preparing. The watercolour is one of many done by John White, whom Ralegh sent out with the first colonists as artist and mapmaker. Seven years earlier White had accompanied Frobisher's expedition in search of the north-west passage and made drawings of the Eskimaux. In Virginia he recorded plants, birds and fish as well as the Indians and their villages, customs and crafts. In 1587 White returned to Virginia as governor of Ralegh's second ill-fated colony.*

driven back by bad weather but Ralegh, eager to show his mettle, remained at sea for another six months.

For a while he continued to be a hanger-on at Court but then, probably with Gilbert's help, came to the notice of some of its leading figures and in particular the Queen's chief favourite, the Earl of Leicester. Through his influence, Ralegh was put in command of a company of troops sent to Ireland in 1580 to help put down a rebellion. He quickly proved himself, not only by reckless courage in action but by his cogent criticism of current policies in Ireland.

It was this, so it was said by contemporaries, that first brought him to the Queen's attention, but later a more romantic explanation was suggested. According to Thomas Fuller's *Worthies of England*: 'Ralegh coming out of Ireland to the English Court in good habit (his clothes then being a considerable part of his estate) found the Queen walking, till meeting with a plashy place, she seemed to scruple walking thereon. Presently Ralegh cast and spread his new plush cloak on the ground, whereon the Queen trod gently, rewarding him afterward with many suits for his so free and seasonable tender of so fair a footcloth.' In reality court etiquette would not have permitted such a casual encounter between the Queen and an unknown gentleman. Most probably Ralegh owed his introduction to Leicester who saw that the Queen would appreciate the young man's dark good looks, enhanced by sumptuous dress, and his spirited conversation. Ralegh quickly joined the inmost circle of courtiers and soon became outstanding among them, 'the Queen's dear minion'. A foreign observer recorded a playful scene between them at this time, in the Presence Chamber at Greenwich: 'She said to a captain named Ralegh, pointing with her finger at his face, that there was smut on it, and was going to wipe it off with her handkerchief, but before she could he wiped it off himself.' Others were as adroit as Ralegh in such byplay, but none could express so well in poetry the homage to

Continued on page 9

SECOTAN

WEAPEMEOC

Dasamonquepeuc

Roanoac

Trinety harbor

Hatorasck

T. B. 2

S · Mil. aur · R
I
H
A
R
D
GRENVILVS
S

Neptuni proles qū magni Martis alumnū
GRENVILVS patrias sanguine tinxit aquas

AN DNI 1602.
ATATIS SVÆ 382

ABOVE LEFT: *Ralegh's first colonising expedition to Virginia arrived off Roanoke Island in July 1585. Only small vessels could get through the shallow passages between the reefs. Larger ships remained dangerously exposed to the open sea. This engraving was made from a watercolour drawing by John White, subsequently lost. In 1590 Theodore de Bry published engravings of all the drawings, together with Thomas Hariot's account of Virginia, at Frankfurt, in English, Latin, French and German. Ralegh's enterprise thus became known throughout Europe.*

FAR LEFT: *Sir Richard Grenville, Ralegh's cousin, shared his interests in privateering, exploration and colonisation. Since the Queen was reluctant to let favourites risk their lives, Ralegh was not allowed to command the expedition to Virginia in 1585 and Grenville went instead. In 1591 he again took Ralegh's place, this time as second-in-command of a fleet intended to intercept the Spanish treasure ships. Off the Azores the English were surprised by Spanish warships. Grenville, ignoring orders, chose to remain and fight. His ship, the* Revenge, *was surrounded, but Grenville fought on until mortally wounded, his crew then surrendering. Ralegh was moved to write a vivid account of the* Revenge's *last fight on which Tennyson based his poem.*

LEFT: *Thomas Hariot was one of the most brilliant mathematicians and astronomers of his time. (He made the first observation of Halley's Comet.) Ralegh established Hariot at Durham House, where he instructed Ralegh and the masters and pilots of his ships, and prepared maps, navigation tables and instruments. In 1585 he accompanied the Virginia colonists. He was to assist Ralegh's later American enterprises and remain a loyal friend. For many, scientific enquiry into the mysteries of the universe was a kind of blasphemy, and Ralegh was to share some of Hariot's reputation for atheism; in fact both were basically orthodox Christians.*

ABOVE RIGHT: *The Strand waterfront, from a panorama of London engraved by C. J. Visscher and published in 1616. Most of the great courtiers had their London houses in this area, conveniently situated between the City and Westminster, and with immediate access to the Thames, the easiest route to the great palaces at Greenwich, Hampton Court, Richmond and Nonsuch. Durham House (the large single-turreted house centre left), once the London house of the Bishops of Durham, had been Crown property throughout the Tudor period and was usually occupied by courtiers or important foreigners. In 1583 Queen Elizabeth gave Ralegh the use of it, rent-free. Twenty years later, after James of Scotland on his way south had been petitioned by the Bishop of Durham for its restitution, Ralegh found himself humiliatingly evicted.*

ABOVE: *Once established at Court, Ralegh began to invest in privateering ventures. More than once captains of his men-of-war went beyond legitimate attacks on the Spanish and he had to justify outright acts of piracy. In 1586 a great warship, the* Ark Ralegh, *was built for him, to a design that included many of his own ideas. But the following year Ralegh presented the ship to the Queen's navy. Renamed the* Ark Royal, *she became the flagship of Lord Admiral Howard and led the English fleet against the Armada. Ralegh had to wait for payment until 1592, when £5000 was written off his debts to the Crown.*

7

ABOVE LEFT: *Ralegh is here portrayed in Greenwich armour as Captain of the Guard. The appointment came in 1587 and made him responsible for the Queen's safety. The portrait is a copy of an original, now lost, probably painted about 1590.*

ABOVE RIGHT: *This portrait, traditionally of Elizabeth Throckmorton, Lady Ralegh, has been regarded as the companion of the portrait of Ralegh in armour, though it was probably painted some 25 years later. The other portrait (page 17) shows her as characterful but decidedly less handsome. Ralegh's poems to her, inspired perhaps by her bold spirit, are full of physical passion. Unlike her husband, she showed no regrets when punishment followed their union.*

LEFT: *Robert Devereux, Earl of Essex, was introduced to the Queen by the Earl of Leicester in 1587. Within two years he had displaced Ralegh as chief favourite, although in 1590 he fell into disgrace when the Queen learned of his marriage. In Sir William Segar's portrait he is probably dressed for the Queen's Accession Day fête in 1590, when he appeared in mourning to implore pardon for his marriage. Once forgiven, he set out to achieve total supremacy at Court, but the Queen found his presumption intolerable. In desperation Essex tried to raise a rebellion in London. He was condemned to death for treason and beheaded at the Tower in February 1601.*

her beauty and majesty that Elizabeth expected:

> Those eyes which set my fancy
> on a fire,
> Those crispèd hairs which hold
> my heart in chains,
> Those dainty hands which
> conquered my desire,
> That wit which of my thought doth
> hold the reins.
>
> Eyes that pierce our hearts
> without remorse,
> Hairs of right that wears a
> royal crown,
> Hands that conquer more than
> Caesar's force,
> Wit that turns huge kingdoms
> upside down.

Ralegh was quickly rewarded. In 1583 he was given the splendid Durham House for his London residence. In 1584 he was granted two of the most profitable monopolies of the time, the 'farm of wines', the Queen's authority to charge every vintner in the kingdom £1 a year for the right to retail wine, and the 'gift of the cloths', a licence to

*　　*　　*

ABOVE RIGHT: *Queen Elizabeth in 1592, the year of Ralegh's disgrace. The portrait, by Marcus Gheeraerts the Younger, discreetly suggests the Queen's ageing features while depicting her as a cosmic figure, standing on a globe of the world (her feet are on Ditchley, the Oxfordshire home of Sir Henry Lee, the courtier who commissioned the picture), on one hand sunshine, symbolising the grace of majesty, on the other storm, to represent the attribute of power. At this very time Ralegh, having basked in the Queen's favour, was now a prisoner in the Tower, struck down by the thunderbolt of her displeasure.*

RIGHT: *While in the Tower Ralegh wrote for the Queen's eyes one of the best-known of all prison poems, which ends: 'Despair bolts up my doors and I alone/Speak to dead walls, but those hear not my moan.' This is one of the few manuscripts of Ralegh's poems to survive in his own hand. Ralegh also began a longer poem on the same theme,* The Book of the Ocean to Cynthia: *the Queen was Cynthia, the moon goddess, Ralegh the Ocean (Elizabeth's nickname for him had been 'Water', a joking reference to his name pronounced in a Devonshire accent), which the moon controls. The poem is a dirge for lost love, and for spent youth and disappointed ambition. While fragmented and obscure, it contains Ralegh's finest and most characteristic poetry.*

9

export undyed woollen broadcloths. In 1584 Ralegh entered the House of Commons, representing the County of Devon, and the next year a series of administrative appointments in Devon and Cornwall made him a leading figure in the region: Lord Warden of the Stannaries (the tin-mining industry), Lord Lieutenant, and Vice-Admiral.

The Queen's favour had made Ralegh one of the richest men in England but, as she intended, he quickly began to spend his new wealth freely in her service. After Sir Humphrey Gilbert had been lost at sea, in 1583, Ralegh took over his leading role in the attempt to found an English colony in America. The small expedition he sent out to explore the coastline of modern North Carolina brought back enthusiastic reports of the area, which Ralegh presented to the Queen. She agreed that the new land should be called Virginia in her honour (as the 'Virgin Queen') and bestowed a knighthood upon him.

In 1585 a hundred settlers were established on Roanoke Island. Although they returned to England after the hardships of their first winter, a second colony was set up in 1587, but when a relief expedition arrived three years later it found the settlement abandoned. Nevertheless Ralegh succeeded in making American colonisation a major national concern, and Virginia became one of the main elements in the Ralegh legend. Soon he was credited with introducing both tobacco and the potato to England from America, although both products were in fact already known through the Spanish.

In the year of the Armada – 1588 – Ralegh was appointed to a select council of war, to advise on national defence, and he now looked forward to establishing himself as a statesman by admission to the Privy Council. But it was not to be. Over-eager to persuade and impress – 'a man that desires to seem to be able to sway all men's fancies, all men's

ABOVE: *Sherborne Castle, now known as the Old Castle and dating largely from the 12th and 13th centuries, had become the residence of the Bishops of Salisbury. After being granted the estate, Ralegh had work carried out at the castle in the expectation of living there (such as new windows and a chimney in the gatehouse), but the buildings proved too dilapidated and he turned his attention to plans for a new residence, on the other side of the River Yeo.*

RIGHT: *Sherborne Lodge, as it was then called, was begun in 1592. At first it was simply a 'tall tower', three storeys high with two main rooms on each floor. The corner turrets, rising another storey, were added in about 1600. The Raleghs' new home was in the forefront of architectural fashion; the lodge—of modest proportion but flamboyant aspect—became widely popular after 1600. Some of the stone used to build the lodge came from the Old Castle (at the top of the picture). The lake between was formed in the 18th century, flooding Ralegh's 'Italian' garden, but on the far side are cedars brought back for him from Virginia.*

RIGHT: *Ralegh in conference with an Indian chief of Guiana, an engraving illustrating Ralegh's account of his expedition in 1595, published by Theodore de Bry in 1599 in his part-work* America. *The friendship of the Indians was vital to Ralegh's plans for an English empire in South America that would rival the Spanish in Peru and Mexico. When he returned to Guiana almost 20 years later, in 1618, he wrote to his wife: 'To tell you that I might be here king of the Indians were a vanity. But my name still lives among them.'*

BELOW: *Ralegh's greatest naval exploit took place during the expedition against Cadiz in 1596, in which he commanded a squadron. The commanders-in-chief were Lord Admiral Howard and Ralegh's successful rival Essex. At Ralegh's persuasion and under his leadership the English attempted to break through the harbour defences to the Spanish merchant fleet within. This contemporary Dutch engraving shows the line of defending oared galleys across the bay, but not the four great galleons which were the first defence. They were driven off after three hours' hard fighting during which Ralegh was struck in the leg by 'a grievous blow, interlaced and deformed with splinters'. Meanwhile English troops had captured Cadiz. The merchant fleet was defenceless and Ralegh was for seizing it. His superiors decided to bargain for a ransom, but the Spanish had the ships fired and scuttled.*

courses' – he was considered unlikely to be a reliable adviser, and too unbending for the give-and-take of committee work. Disappointed of a seat on the Council, Ralegh now found his position at Court challenged by the young Earl of Essex, as Elizabeth, conscious of advancing years, desperately seized the opportunity to renew her youth by playing the game of courtly love with a new admirer. Ralegh had not altogether lost the Queen's favour, however, and it was at this time that she conferred on him the lease of Sherborne Castle in north Dorset, the West Country estate he had wanted for so long.

Even while the Queen's chief favour-

*   *   *

ABOVE: *Sherborne Castle, from the south. The wings with turrets extending out from Ralegh's lodge were added in about 1625, by John Digby, Earl of Bristol, to whom James I had granted the Sherborne estate eight years before. The castle remains with the Digby family to this day.*

ite, Ralegh had been discreetly carrying on flirtations or affairs at Court. Earlier, in Ireland, he had had a daughter by one Alice Goold, and continued to take an interest in her welfare. Now, displaced by Essex, Ralegh was ready to seek fuller satisfactions than he could find in public courtship of the ageing Queen and casual intrigues. He began to woo Bess Throckmorton, one of the Queen's ladies-in-waiting, at 26 some dozen years younger than himself:

> Now Serena be not coy;
> Since we freely may enjoy
> Sweet embraces: such delights
> As will shorten tedious nights.

A child was conceived and, probably in November 1591, the couple were secretly married. Rumours began to spread. Ralegh knew that they would have to face Elizabeth's anger when she learned of the affair, for she had shown her resentment at the marriages of other favourites. The only way to appease the Queen would have been to admit the

deception and beg forgiveness. But Ralegh's pride would not allow this. Instead, he hoped to win a pardon by some spectacular action against Spain, to the Queen's profit. As Bess awaited the birth of their child Ralegh was busy preparing an expedition against Panama

*   *   *

RIGHT: *Ralegh and his elder son Wat, in 1602. The boy was then aged about nine. Although denied a place in the Privy Council, Ralegh became re-established as a leading figure at Court in close attendance on the Queen as Captain of the Guard. Robert Cecil, the chief minister, was anxious for his goodwill. Ralegh was appointed Governor of Jersey, an important strategic command; as Warden of the Stannaries he was given the monopoly of tin produced in Devon and Cornwall for resale on the London market; and his lease of Sherborne was converted into a perpetual grant. Ralegh was also taking a leading part in the House of Commons, in his own right as an experienced parliamentarian.*

SERO SED SERIO

to which the Queen had contributed. Ralegh was to be in command, but at the last moment Elizabeth decided he was to accompany the fleet only as far as the coast of Spain. While Ralegh was at sea the news of his secret marriage reached the Queen, and shortly after his return he and Bess were put in custody. Soon they were sent to the Tower of London, to be kept apart as 'close' prisoners.

Now, too late, Ralegh affected extravagant grief and self-abasement. 'My heart was never broken till this day', he wrote to Robert Cecil in a letter meant for Elizabeth, 'that I hear the Queen goes away so far off, whom I have followed so many years with great love and desire, in so many journeys, and am now left behind her, in a dark prison cell alone . . .' The Queen was unmoved. Only when Ralegh was needed for her service was he released. The expedition from which he had been called back had taken a prize of immense value, a Portuguese ship from the East Indies loaded with spices and silks, which had been brought into Dartmouth. Ralegh, still in custody, was sent down to safeguard the Queen's share, while forfeiting to her, in effect as his ransom, the larger share that was due to him. At the end of the year 1592 he and Bess were released from the Tower.

Excluded from Court, Ralegh and his wife began a new life centred on Sherborne. He began to renovate the old castle, but soon changed his plans and had a fine new residence constructed nearby. The Raleghs' first son had died in infancy but their second was born in 1594, and given his father's name. But Ralegh could never be content with domestic life and soon he was scheming to recover the Queen's favour. For several years Ralegh had been gathering information about the region of South America known as Guiana, now Venezuela, and particularly about the fabled empire of El Dorado, which the English called Manoa, in the Guiana Highlands. In 1595 he set off in command of an expedition that was intended to lay the foundations of an English empire in South America.

Ralegh returned convinced that the Indians were eager to join the English against their Spanish oppressors and would happily accept the protection of Queen Elizabeth, that El Dorado was a reality, and that there was gold-bearing ore in abundance to be found beside the Orinoco river. He quickly wrote *The Discovery of the Large, Rich and Beautiful Empire of Guiana*, hoping that the

FACING PAGE, ABOVE: *Robert Cecil was primarily responsible for Ralegh's downfall, so as to secure his own position with James I and ensure peace with Spain. Once Ralegh was in the Tower, however, Cecil helped protect the interests of his family. On his arrival in England King James raised Cecil to the peerage and in 1605 he became Earl of Salisbury. John de Critz the Elder's portrait dates from 1602.*

FACING PAGE, BELOW: *Henry Howard, Ralegh's bitterest enemy. He privately supported Mary Queen of Scots' claim to the English throne, and became a trusted informant of her son. Thanks mainly to him, James arrived in England convinced that Ralegh was his secret enemy. Soon made Earl of Northampton, Howard had the satisfaction of being a judge at Ralegh's trial.*

ABOVE: *Henry Brooke, Lord Cobham, became Ralegh's closest associate in the last years of Elizabeth's reign. Cobham, while ambitious, lacked any political sense and Ralegh unwisely let himself be drawn into his intrigues. Charged with treason, Cobham lost his nerve and, to save his skin, helped prepare the case against Ralegh. Spared execution, Cobham died after 15 years in the Tower.*

Queen would send out an expedition with himself in command to annex and govern it; 'the shining glory of this conquest will eclipse all those so far extended beams of the Spanish nation. . . . whatsoever prince shall possess it shall be the greatest . . .' But even Ralegh's eloquent prose could not persuade the Queen to share his hopes of Guiana.

Soon after Ralegh's return a great expedition was mounted against Cadiz. He was given command of one of the squadrons and played a leading part in the action. In the spring of 1597 he was received back into favour by the Queen. The Court was now divided by the rivalry between Essex and Robert Cecil, the younger son of Lord Burleigh and his intended successor as chief minister. At first, to Cecil's alarm, Ralegh and Essex worked closely together to hasten preparations for a new expedition, which was to intercept the Spanish treasure fleet off the Azores. In the event, largely owing to Essex's mismanagement, nothing was achieved except the capture of the town of Fayal, which was carried out by Ralegh, who had led his men ashore

*   *   *

ABOVE LEFT: *James I in 1606, by John de Critz the Elder, the King's Sergeant Painter. James had been prejudiced against Ralegh by the reports of Robert Cecil and Henry Howard, who had represented him as a secret enemy. If John Aubrey, the 17th-century antiquary and gossip, is to be believed, at their first meeting Ralegh confirmed James's worst suspicions: when James boasted that if the English had tried to keep him out he would by his own strength have secured the Crown, Ralegh replied, 'Would to God that had been put to the trial . . . then you would have known your friends from your foes.' James was soon persuaded that Ralegh, with Cobham, had been plotting to depose him in favour of his cousin Lady Arabella Stuart.*

LEFT: *In this room, above the gatehall of the Bloody Tower, Ralegh wrote his* History of the World, *and numerous essays on politics, strategy, shipping and philosophy, during his 12 years' imprisonment. Substantial changes were made for the convenience of the Raleghs: an upper chamber was even created by inserting a floor, making the tower higher and putting in a new upper window. This room has been restored as a bedchamber but in his later years Ralegh preferred to sleep in his 'garden house', an extension to the shed in which he conducted his experiments.*

16

under fire through heavy surf. Essex's jealousy and suspicion of his old rival were rekindled, and when his downfall came three years later he mistakenly saw Ralegh as largely responsible.

With Robert Cecil in total command Ralegh felt his fortunes were at a stand and he began to associate with Cecil's malcontent brother-in-law, Lord Cobham. Cecil could be sure of his supremacy only so long as Elizabeth lived, and in 1601 he began a correspondence with her obvious successor, James VI of Scotland. Cobham too was trying to establish himself with James. Cecil, believing Ralegh a party to his intrigues, set about discrediting him with James although in fact Ralegh chose to stand aloof from such politicking.

When, following Elizabeth's death in March 1603, James arrived in England, he greeted Ralegh, if tradition is to be believed, with an ominous pun: 'O my soul mon, I have heard rawly of thee.' At a second audience, hoping to impress James as statesman and strategist, Ralegh presented a 'Discourse concerning a war with Spain'. Cecil was much alarmed, for he was determined on peace

*   *   *

ABOVE RIGHT: *Henry Percy, ninth Earl of Northumberland and Ralegh's close friend, became a fellow-prisoner in 1605 when convicted of complicity in the Gunpowder Plot. He shared Ralegh's scientific interests and had taken his place as the patron of Hariot and other scholars whom Ralegh had maintained before his disgrace. One of England's wealthiest men, he lived in great magnificence in the Tower, laying out walks and a bowling alley next to his lodgings in the Martin Tower, and a 'still-house' for his experiments. Northumberland was released in 1621, departing to a salute from the Tower guns. The portrait, painted after his death in 1632, is by Van Dyck.*

RIGHT: *This portrait, said to be Lady Ralegh's, bears the date 1605 though the costume suggests 1600 or earlier and the sitter's age is given as 35 whereas Lady Ralegh would have been 40. During her husband's imprisonment Bess had to take the responsibility for bringing up their two sons and protecting the family interests. After one visit from her Ralegh wrote, 'I shall be made more than weary of my life by her crying and bewailing . . . She hath already brought her eldest son in one hand and her sucking child in another, crying out of her and their destruction, charging me with unnatural negligence.' Despite these stresses Bess was to live till 82.*

17

asunder; and God hath divided me from the world, and you from me.' But it was not the end. Royal justice having been executed on some of the plotters in a related conspiracy, James was now ready to extend the royal mercy to Ralegh and Cobham and win credit for his magnanimity.

For more than 12 years Ralegh remained in the Tower. If not 'lodged and attended as well in the Tower as in his house', as Robert Cecil claimed, he was treated with consideration. He had the use of the Bloody Tower and the adjoining garden. Three servants lived in and a physician and a clergyman regularly attended him. His wife and son visited him every day, even stayed with him. A second son was born in 1605, and christened Carew in St Peter's Chapel on the Green. There was an unending flow of visitors including some Indians brought back by Ralegh from Guiana 10 years before, who came for instruction in English. He had a hut in the garden made into a chemical laboratory and from herbs and shrubs which he grew distilled medical cordials that were to become widely celebrated.

But Ralegh's health was worsening in the damp and cold beside the river, and after three years he suffered a severe stroke. Family affairs too were a constant vexation. In the normal course a traitor's assets were confiscated to the Crown, but Ralegh was confident that Sherborne was safe, having transferred the title to his elder son. But on examination of the deed it was found that the crucial words required to effect the transfer had been left out, and in 1607 Sherborne was lost, when King James took it for his new favourite Robert Carr.

Yet, coming at that time, the blow was less hard to bear. For in this same year the Queen, Anne of Denmark, having visited Ralegh to obtain one of his cordials, returned with her eldest son, Prince Henry, then aged 13, and Ralegh, the convicted traitor, became in effect tutor to the heir to the throne. For Henry, Ralegh began his masterpiece *The History of the World*, to help the boy prepare himself for kingship. It was as yet too soon to hope for a pardon, but in anticipation of that day the Prince got his father to persuade Robert Carr to give up Sherborne to him, to be held in trust for Ralegh. But late that same year, 1612, all Ralegh's hopes, for himself and his country, were dashed at one blow. Prince Henry was taken ill with typhoid. With the King's physicians despairing of his recovery, one of Ralegh's cordials was even administered, but in vain.

with Spain and not yet sure of James's attitude, though the King was soon to seize eagerly on the role of peacemaker. At this juncture, happily for Cecil, Cobham's activities gave him the opportunity to be rid of Ralegh for good.

In July 1603 Ralegh was put under arrest and shortly after was sent to the Tower, on suspicion of high treason. It was alleged that he had encouraged Cobham to propose to the Spanish a plot to dethrone James in favour of his English cousin, Arabella Stuart. In fact, Ralegh was involved only in that he knew from Cobham what was afoot and had even received from him, though he did not accept, an offer of Spanish money. There seemed no escape for Ralegh from the shame of a traitor's death. 'I never saw so strange a dejected mind', the Lieutenant of the Tower reported, and a few days after Ralegh tried to take his own life, by thrusting a table knife into his chest. But the point was stopped by a rib, and he suffered only a gash which healed quickly. Seeing his escape from self-destruction as providential, Ralegh was seized by the hope that he might still establish his innocence. Cobham too was a prisoner in the Tower, and Ralegh found ways to communicate with him; one letter was tied to an apple which was thrown in at Cobham's window. Cobham passed back a letter which affirmed Ralegh's complete innocence, but he then informed the government and disowned what he had written to Ralegh.

Ralegh was taken down to Winchester for trial. He easily exposed the absurdity of the essential case against him, that he had a 'Spanish heart', thereby laying the foundation for his popular reputation as a patriotic hero, but he could not refute the charges against him. Ralegh was relying on the letter in which Cobham exonerated him from any part in the conspiracy, but before he could produce it the prosecutor read out the retraction Cobham had written immediately afterwards. The verdict of guilty, from a packed jury, was a foregone conclusion. Returned to the Tower, Ralegh composed himself for death. He wrote to his wife. 'My love I send you, that you may keep it when I am dead; and my counsel, that you may remember it when I am no more . . . Death hath cut us

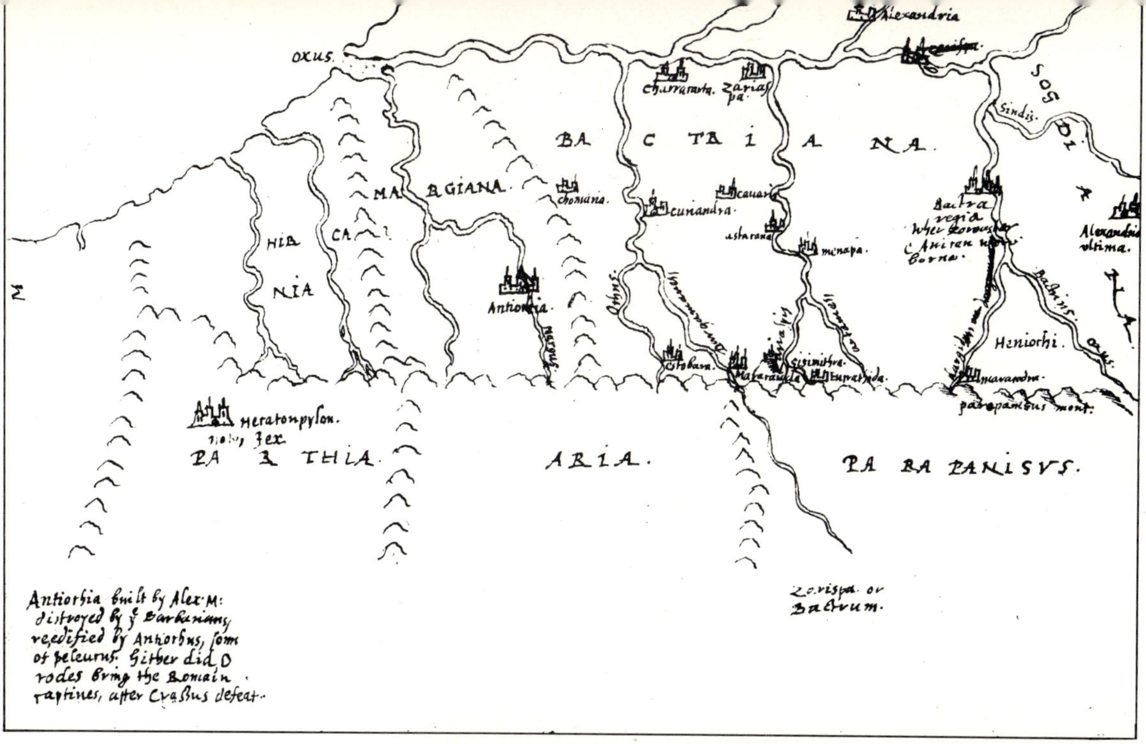

The map at the top of the page contains the following labels:

OXUS.

Alexandria

Charramata. Zariaspa

BA C T RI A NA

Oxos

MARGIANA

chomana

Sindis

Scuriandra

Scauari

astarana

menapa

Bactra regia ubi thesaur C Aniten Corna

Alexandria ultima

HIBCANIA

Anhoria

Henioti

Ochana

Maracula

Bupasuda

Sisimithra

muavandra

paropanisus mont.

Heratonpylon.
noly Hex.

PA R THIA

ARIA.

PA RA PANISVS.

Antiorhia built by Alex M:
distroyed by y barbarians,
reedified by Anhorbus, son
of seleurus. Sither did D
rodes bring the Romain
raptines, after Crassus defeat.

Zorispa or
Bactrum.

FACING PAGE: *When Sir William Waad was appointed Lieutenant of the Tower in 1605 he was much dismayed by Ralegh's accessibility to casual visitors and had a high brick wall built around the garden adjoining the Bloody Tower where Ralegh spent much of his day. He also put a stop to Lady Ralegh bringing her coach into the Tower when visiting her husband. But even Waad could not hinder Ralegh's most distinguished visitors, King James's queen and his heir.*

ABOVE: *A page of notes in Ralegh's hand for his* History of the World, *which he began in 1608–9 and broke off in 1612, after the death of Prince Henry. In preparing the work Ralegh read widely, borrowing books and manuscripts from his friends, and the* History *cites some 500 authors in several languages. This page comes from a notebook in which Ralegh began an index of his geographical notes to use in his study of Old Testament history, perhaps as early as the 1590s when he may have conceived the idea of the* History.

RIGHT: *Ben Jonson was at the height of his fame as playwright and man of letters when in 1613 he accompanied Ralegh's elder son to Paris. Ralegh, after his own wild youth, proved a conventional father, who was much dismayed by Wat's pranks. He had sent him to Oxford where he had three years at Corpus Christi College, and now hoped that foreign travel under the tutelage of the learned Jonson might polish his manners. But Jonson was too convivial for such responsibility. In Paris Wat got him drunk and then had him drawn on a cart through the streets, telling passers-by 'that was a more lively image of the crucifix than any they had'.*

After the Prince's death Ralegh completed the first part of his *History*, from the Creation to the year 133 BC, but abandoned the second and third volumes he had planned. The book was published in 1614, but within a few months was suppressed. The King, it was said, had found it 'too saucy in censuring princes'. Ralegh had commented scathingly on a number of rulers whom the reader was likely to identify with James himself, such as King Ninias of Assyria, 'esteemed no man of war at all, but altogether feminine, and subjected to ease and delicacy', and the central thesis of the work was that God held rulers to account for the government of their people and that his judgements upon them were carried out by human hands. At the same time, in the *History* Ralegh comes to terms with his own fate: '. . . the world's bright glory hath put out the eyes of our minds . . . It is therefore Death alone that can suddenly make man to know himself. He tells the proud and insolent, that they are but abjects, and humbles them at the instant . . .'

During 1615, for the first time, James began to consider Ralegh's Guiana scheme. He had been seeking to marry his heir, Charles, to the King of Spain's daughter, but the Spanish insisted on impossible conditions. By allowing Ralegh to proceed, James might make the Spanish realise that his friendship could not be taken for granted, while if they still would not compromise Guiana gold might help solve the King's financial problems instead of the Spanish dowry he had looked for. In March 1616 Ralegh was released from the Tower. Though in his sixties and still suffering the effects of another severe stroke the previous year, he set to work vigorously and a formidable force was assembled. The Spanish grew alarmed and, to placate them, James privately agreed that Ralegh's life should be forfeit if he clashed with the Spanish in Guiana.

Ralegh arrived at the mouth of the Orinoco at the end of 1617. He had fallen ill on the voyage, and it was Lawrence Keymis who led the party up river. Ralegh's elder son, Wat, went with him. Ralegh had directed Keymis to seek out the gold mine while avoiding hostilities against the Spanish unless he were attacked. But Keymis continued up the Orinoco until he arrived before the Spanish fort of San Thomé. Either he had lost his way, or he had a plan of his own. At nightfall his troops landed and soon blundered into a Spanish patrol. Young Wat Ralegh ran forward to rally the waverers. He was fatally wounded by a musket shot, but the English charged on to storm San Thomé. The way was now open to the mine, but Keymis found himself at a loss. He had no charts of the area and the old landmarks had gone. After a few half-hearted attempts he led his party back to the coast. Ralegh, sweeping aside all his excuses, mercilessly berated him, and Keymis, rejected by the leader he had served loyally, stabbed himself to the heart. Ralegh wanted to go in search of the mine himself but his men would not follow him, and he began the voyage homeward. In a letter to his wife, Ralegh poured out his despair: 'As Sir Francis Drake and Sir John Hawkins died broken-hearted when they failed of their enterprise, I would willingly do the like, did I not contend against sorrow, in hope to provide somewhat for you in comfort and relieve you . . .'

From the time that he learned of Keymis's failure until the eve of his execution six months later, Ralegh was a prey to conflicting emotions: should he seek to escape a shameful traitor's death and go into exile, hoping to find some new enterprise that would restore his reputation? Or should he try to justify what had happened, clear his name and persuade the King to mercy? In fact from the beginning James was resolved that Ralegh should die, for Spain had demanded it as the test of his friendship. For a time Ralegh was left at liberty, to give him time and encouragement to discredit himself and lose public sympathy. He was finally arrested on his way down the Thames to a ship waiting to take him to France. For the last time he was brought to the Tower.

Just as when Ralegh had been awaiting trial for treason his thoughts turned to suicide, but this time he brushed them aside and resolved 'to die in the light not in the darkness', for at last he saw his course clear: to vindicate himself before the world and make a good death. He was already a condemned man, under the death sentence passed at Winchester 15 years before. The execution was fixed for 29 October 1618, in Old Palace Yard, Westminster.

Ralegh was lodged overnight in the Abbey Gatehouse. There he took his farewell of friends and relatives. His last visitor was his wife. She had spent the day seeking a reprieve but had come away only with permission to arrange for the burial of her husband's body. 'It is as well, dear Bess,' he replied to the news, 'that thou mayest dispose of it dead, that hadst not always the dispos-
Continued on page 24

FACING PAGE, ABOVE: *Anne of Denmark, James I's queen, first visited Ralegh in the Tower in 1607 when she came to collect some of his Balsam of Guiana, a cordial of strawberry water. Impressed and charmed by his conversation (no one at her husband's court had such distinction and style), Anne returned with her son Prince Henry, whose friendship gave Ralegh new hope in his imprisonment. But despite her goodwill there was nothing else she could do for him. James was influenced only by his favourites, never by his wife. This portrait, by Gheeraerts the Younger, dates from about 1605–10.*

FACING PAGE, BELOW: *'No one but my father would keep such a bird in a cage', commented Henry, Prince of Wales, who became Ralegh's pupil in the last five years of his life. He deliberately set himself apart from his father's court, instead patronising the culture of chivalry that had flourished around Queen Elizabeth. In contrast to his timid, ungainly father, Henry fought in the tournament and studied the art of war. Ralegh saw in him not only the best hope for his release but the prospect of England returning to a spirited foreign policy that would contest Spain's ambition to dominate both Europe and America. He wrote essays for the Prince on foreign policy and encouraged his in-*

terest in the navy. Above all, he began his History of the World *'for the service of that inestimable Prince Henry, the successive hope, and one of the greatest of the Christian world'. The portrait, a miniature by Isaac Oliver, dates from about two years before Henry's untimely death.*

ABOVE: *Robert Carr became James I's chief favourite early in the reign and was created Earl of Somerset. To support his new rank he needed a landed estate, and at this time it was confirmed that Sherborne was forfeit to the Crown because of Ralegh's treason. Despite Lady Ralegh's tearful protests, James decided, 'I maun hae the land; I maun hae it for Carr.' However, he was gracious enough to allow Lady Ralegh generous compensation. The Raleghs were to be revenged, for in 1616, after Sir Walter's release, Carr was brought a prisoner to the Bloody Tower, having been convicted of complicity in the murder of his former friend Sir Thomas Overbury, who had been poisoned while a prisoner in the Tower, with the connivance of the Lieutenant, Sir Gervase Elwes. Carr's wife, Frances Howard, who had instigated the crime, was imprisoned in Ralegh's garden house. The couple remained in the Tower for six years. Sherborne passed from Carr to Sir John Digby, who had been ambassador in Madrid.*

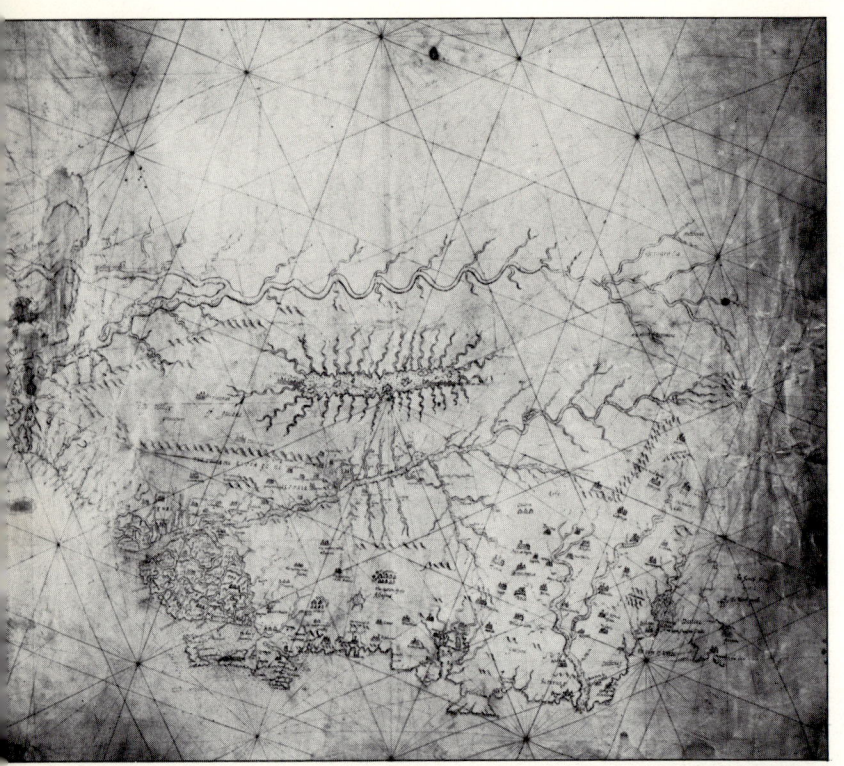

LEFT: *A map of Guiana, probably prepared for Ralegh after his expedition in 1595 by Thomas Hariot. The coast is at the bottom and the Orinoco runs across from left to right. At the top El Dorado is marked at one end of a great inland sea, the Lake of Manoa. There was in fact no lake but the area was regularly flooded during the rainy season. While Ralegh was in the Tower other English explorers tried but failed to locate El Dorado, and when Ralegh proposed his second expedition he made no reference to it, instead concentrating on the gold mine of which he claimed first-hand knowledge.*

BELOW LEFT: *Ralegh is portrayed in an engraving by Simon van de Passe as commander of his forthcoming Guiana expedition in 1617 on the title page of the second edition of* The History of the World. *The book's first edition had appeared in 1614 without Ralegh's name on the title page; as a convicted traitor he was in law a non-person.*

BELOW RIGHT: *Wat Ralegh portrayed after his death, with a picture of the attack on the Spanish fort of San Thomé in which he was killed. He had come back to join his father's expedition from the Netherlands where he had fled after wounding a man in a duel. By a terrible irony Wat helped seal his father's fate, for the capture of San Thomé which he inspired was a flagrant breach of Ralegh's undertaking not to attack the Spanish.*

VERA EFFIGIES CLARISS. VIRI DOM IN GUALTHERI RALEGH EQV. AUR. &c.

The true and lively portraiture of the honourable and learned Knight Sʳ Walter Ralegh.

AMORE ET VIRTVTE

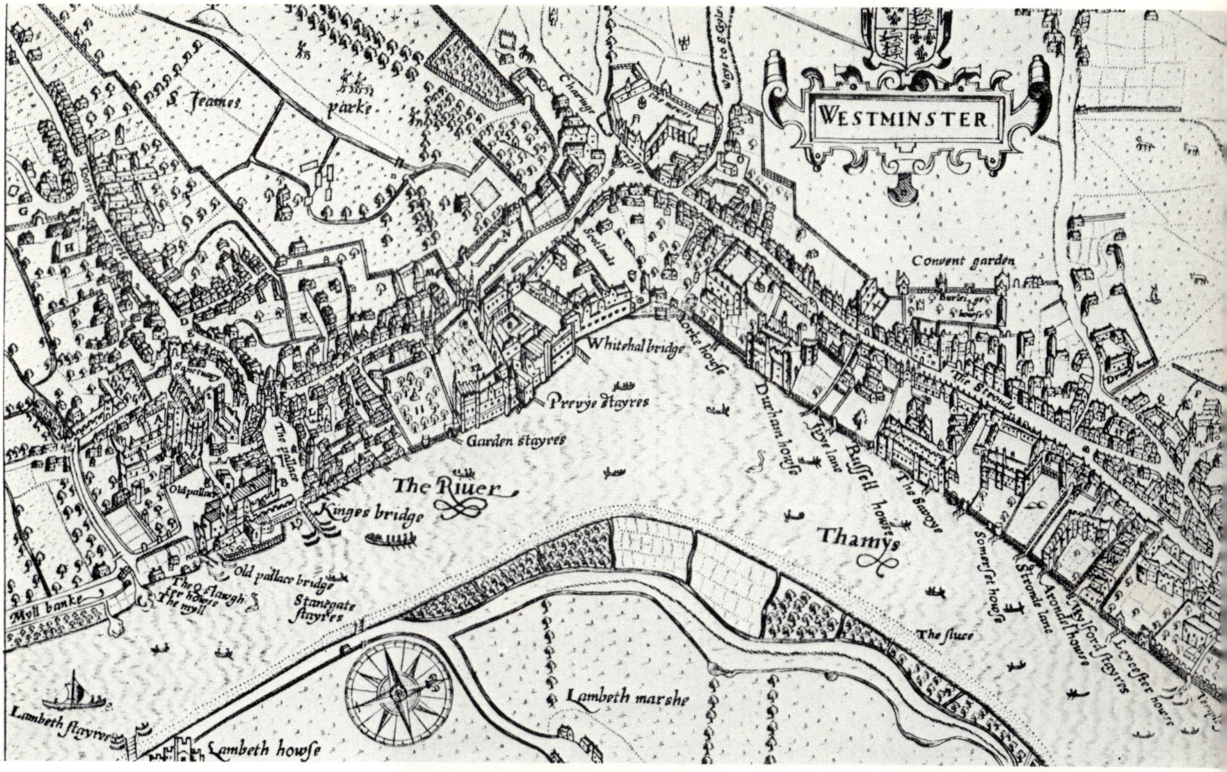

The map of Westminster at the top of the page shows the River Thames with labelled locations including *Westminster*, *Convent garden*, *Whitehal bridge*, *Prevye stayres*, *Garden stayres*, *The Ryver*, *Kinges bridge*, *Old pallace bridge*, *Stangate stayres*, *Moll banke*, *The sluce*, *Thamys*, *Lambeth marshe*, *Lambeth stayres*, and *Lambeth howse*. River-side buildings are labelled *Yorke howse*, *Durham howse*, *Bye ime*, *Ruffll howse*, *The Savoy*, *Somerset howse*, *Strond ine*, *Arundll howse*, *Leyther howse*.

ABOVE: *In October 1618 Ralegh was brought from the Tower to Westminster Hall, before the judges of the King's Bench. They ruled that the death sentence imposed 15 years before be carried out in view of his further offences against the King. Ralegh was lodged overnight in the Gatehouse of Westminster Abbey that led into the Sanctuary, and the next day went out to the scaffold in Old Palace Yard. His body was buried in St Margaret's Church beside the Abbey. This map of Westminster, from John Norden's* Speculum Britanniae, *also contains reminders of Ralegh's happier days, the Palace of Whitehall where Elizabeth usually held court during the winter and his residence at Durham House.*

RIGHT: *The formidable Count Gondomar, Spanish ambassador in London, was unable to prevent Ralegh's expedition to Guiana. But he got from King James the promise that if Ralegh did any harm to Spanish subjects or their property he would be sent to Madrid for punishment. James also supplied Gondomar with full details of the expedition and its intended route, which were passed on to the Spanish authorities in Guiana. When Ralegh returned Gondomar demanded that the 'pirate' should be handed over as James had promised. The King was ready to agree but his ministers dissuaded him, knowing that such subservience would have outraged public opinion. The portrait is by Abraham Blijenbergh.*

severed. Ralegh's body was buried in St Margaret's Church nearby; his head was taken away in a red velvet bag by Lady Ralegh. Later it passed into the possession of their son Carew, and was probably buried with him.

As Ralegh had intended, the manner of his death vindicated not only the man but his cause – the Crown at one with the nation, vigorously asserting England's interests abroad. That to his mind was the ideal which Elizabeth had fulfilled and James betrayed. Among the crowd who heard Ralegh speak and saw him die were men who were to be the foremost leaders of the parliamentary opposition to James's son Charles I, Sir John Eliot and John Pym, and many of their followers were to be influenced by the accounts of that day and by Ralegh's writings. Ralegh had failed in all his great ambitions and enterprises, but by his deeds and words had captured the imagination of his fellow-countrymen. In death he achieved that influence on England's destiny he had been denied in life.

*   *   *

ACKNOWLEDGMENTS

The illustrations are acknowledged as follows: front cover, pp 4 (bottom), 9 (top), 13, 14 (top), 19 (bottom) and 21, reproduced by kind permission of the Trustees, National Portrait Gallery, London; inside cover, pp 8 (top left), 10 (top) and 16 (bottom), Department of the Environment, Crown copyright reserved; p 1, Mr Simon Wingfield Digby, Sherborne Castle; pp 2 (both), 6 (top and bottom left), 11 (top), 18, 19 (top) and 22 (top and bottom left), reproduced by permission of the British Library Board; p 3, from the collection at Parham Park, Sussex; p 4 (top), photograph by Nicholas Servian, F.I.I.P., Woodmansterne Ltd; pp 5 (top) and 9 (bottom), by courtesy of the Marquess of Salisbury; pp 5 (bottom) and 7 (both), reproduced by courtesy of the Trustees of the British Museum; p 6 (bottom right), by courtesy of the President and Fellows of Trinity College, Oxford; p 8 (top), Colonial Williamsburg photograph; pp 8 (bottom), 17 (bottom) and back cover, courtesy of the National Gallery of Ireland; p 10 (bottom), Aerofilms Ltd; p 11 (bottom), by permission of the Trustees of the National Maritime Museum, Greenwich; p 12, photograph by Clive Friend, F.I.I.P., Woodmansterne Ltd; p 14 (bottom), from the collection of Lord Egremont (photograph by the Courtauld Institute of Art); p 15, Sir Hugo Boothby, Bt (photograph by the National Museum of Wales, Cardiff); p 16 (top), Dulwich College; p 17 (top), Petworth House, a property of the National Trust; p 20 (top), by kind permission of the Marquess of Tavistock and the Trustees of the Bedford Estates, Woburn Abbey; pp 20 (bottom) and 23 (bottom), reproduced by gracious permission of Her Majesty The Queen; pp 22 (bottom right) and 24, by permission of His Grace The Duke of Rutland, C.B.E. (photograph on p 22 from the Mansell Collection); p 23 (top), Guildhall, London.

ing of it when alive.' The next morning Ralegh received Holy Communion, ate a good breakfast and smoked a pipe. A great crowd had gathered around the scaffold, and Ralegh was ready for them.

*   *   *

ABOVE: *Ralegh appears as at the end of his life but the inset scene shows what was perhaps his most heroic exploit, the capture of Fayal in the Azores, more than 20 years before. Lady Ralegh is said to have commissioned this miniature after his death, together with one of their elder son Wat (page 22), and had them cased in a locket.*

He had dressed with his old elegance, and carefully rehearsed his last words. It was perhaps the longest speech ever to be delivered from the scaffold, lasting some three-quarters of an hour, but then few prisoners ever had such a sympathetic audience. He declined the offer of a blindfold. 'Think you I fear the shadow of the axe, when I fear not the axe itself?' He laid his head on the block, and having prayed, put out his hands as a signal for the axe to descend. But the headsman hesitated. 'What dost thou fear? Strike, man, strike!' The axe fell, once, twice, before the neck was

ISBN 85372 257 9